The Es

C. P. Cavafy

BORN 1863
DIED 1933

The Essential
CAVAFY

Selected and with an
Introduction by

EDMUND KEELEY

Translated by
Edmund Keeley and Philip Sherrard
Notes by George Savidis

The Ecco Press

The translations selected here (with the exception of "The Ships") are from the revised edition of C.P. Cavafy: Collected Poems, translated by Edmund Keeley and Philip Sherrard, Princeton University Press, 1992.

The notes by George Savidis (with the exception of that to "The Ships") are from the same edition. The introduction by Edmund Keeley draws in part on themes explored more fully in his Cavafy's Alexandria, Princeton University Press, 1995.

THE ECCO PRESS
100 West Broad Street
Hopewell, New Jersey 08525
Published simultaneously in Canada by
Penguin Books Canada Ltd., Ontario
Printed in the United States of America

Library of Congress Cataloging-in-Publication Data

Cavafy, Constantine, 1863–1933.
[Selections. English. 1995]
The essential Cavafy / selected and with an introduction by Edmund
Keeley ; translated by Edmund Keeley and Philip Sherrard ; notes by
George Savidis.
p. cm.—(The essential poets series ; 22)
"The translations [and notes] selected here (with the exception of
"The ships") are from the revised edition of C.P. Cavafy : collected
poems ... Princeton University Press, 1992"—CIP front matter.
ISBN 0-88001-426-1
ISBN 0-88001-516-0 (pbk)
1. Cavafy, Constantine, 1863–1933—Translations, English.
I. Keeley, Edmund. II. Sherrard, Philip. III. Cavafy, Constantine,
1863–1933. C.P. Cavafy. IV. Title. V. Series: Essential Poets ; 22
PA5610.K2A24 1995
899'.132—dc20 95-8451

Contents

❖❖

The Essential Cavafy

Introduction

❖

The essential thing about C. P. Cavafy, most of his early commentators agreed, was his uniqueness—and this was said before the term became a descriptive cliché. E. M. Forster, the first of his British admirers along with T. E. Lawrence and Arnold Toynbee, defined Cavafy's attitude, after meeting the Alexandrian during World War I, in the now-famous phrase that distinguished Cavafy from his contemporaries: this poet stood "at a slight angle to the universe." Some twenty years after the poet's death in 1933, W. H. Auden spoke of Cavafy's "unique perspective on the world" and his "unique tone of voice." And what George Seferis, his first truly perceptive Greek critic, found unique about him was that, great as many of his mature poems proved to be, no one could have predicted on the basis of his earliest work that he had sufficient talent to be regarded in due course as a poet of substance, let alone the most important poet of the twentieth century writing in Greek. What even Seferis could not have predicted was that, by the last decade of the century, Cavafy would come to be so regarded not only in Greece but wherever his work was broadly translated. Auden anticipated this development when he indicated that one proof of Cavafy's uniqueness was the apparent capacity of his work to survive translation, so that the reader who has no Greek still feels on reading a poem by Cavafy that "nobody else could possibly have written it."

Those who look to the surface of a life for signs of genius would also have had trouble predicting Cavafy's posthumous celebrity, even if there were aspects of that life that seemed unique as well. For one, though a poet sublimely erudite in Greek history and well-read first in English and then in French literature, he had almost no formal education that appears in the record beyond a brief period in an Alexandrian commercial school. And though cosmopolitan in his outlook, after he committed himself to poetry he rarely left his native city of Alexandria to travel elsewhere, in fact spent most of his mature years working as a clerk in the Irrigation Service of the local Ministry of Public Works. We learn from Robert Liddell's biography that Cavafy was the youngest of nine siblings and that he lived with his mother until her death in 1899 (he was thirty-five), then for a while with his brother Paul, and during his last twenty-five years, alone in the same second-floor apartment on a street (Rue Lepsius) that was considerably less fashionable than what his parents had been accustomed to before the collapse of Cavafy Brothers, the family's once-lucrative export-import firm. The apartment, now a museum honoring the poet, has a balcony overlooking streets that in those days belonged to an old Greek quarter with both a respectable and an ill-famed aspect: a hospital, the patriarchal church of St. Sava, and on the ground floor of Cavafy's building, a brothel. The poet was reported to have said: "Where could I live better? Below, the brothel caters for the flesh. And there is the church which forgives sin. And there is the hospital where we die."

Though the choice of Alexandria for a restricted life proved essential for the poetry, Cavafy did not choose it easily. As late as 1907, when the poet was forty-four, he was still tormented by the prospect of remaining in the same city: "By now I've gotten used to Alexandria," he writes in a note to himself, "and it's very likely that even if I were rich I'd stay here. But in spite of this, how the place disturbs me. What trouble, what a burden small cities are—what lack of freedom. I'd stay here (then again I'm not entirely certain that I'd stay) because it is like a native country for me, because it is related to my life's memories. But how much a man like me—so different—needs a large city. London, let's say. . . . " As a homosexual with limited resources living in a society that one poem calls "prudish and stupid" ("Days of 1896"), Cavafy clearly felt confined by the "small corner" of the world that torments the speaker in the 1910 poem "The City." At the same time, as the home of his "life's memories," Alexandria soon became the primary source for poem after poem that invoked, through memory, the more or less secret erotic experience of his youth that he decided to reveal with growing candor and verisimilitude. And by 1910, three years after his ambivalent note to himself and after he had settled into the Rue Lepsius apartment for the rest of his life, signaling his accommodation with the city, Alexandria began to be transformed in the central "historical" myth of his mature work.

This development of both an increasingly free exploitation of his youthful eroticism and an inventive exploitation of his city's history from Hellenistic times through the Arab conquest emerged from a turning point in his understanding of his vocation as a poet. Cavafy himself marked the date by dividing his poems into those published before 1911 and those published after. By that date he had decided to put aside most of what he had written during the previous decades, over 200 poems, and to preserve only 24 (among them one of his most famous, "Waiting for the Barbarians") that would join another 130 that he wrote in subsequent years, the so-called Cavafy canon: wrote but did not publish in the usual way. One aspect of Cavafy's aspiration to write as he chose, without concern for the society of his day and its marketplace, was his idiosyncratic mode of promulgating his work. He never offered a volume of poems for sale during his lifetime. And a number of good poems of his maturity actually remained unpublished in any form, kept among his papers for possible revision at some later date (five of the six translations that conclude this selection are of poems recovered from Cavafy's papers by George Savidis). Those poems that Cavafy allowed to be printed during his lifetime were distributed to a restricted audience. He would pass them out as they seemed ready to his trusted friends first in sample pamphlets, then as broadsheets and offprints, these usually gathered into folders that could be supplemented regularly, some of the older poems revised by hand now and then, a few suppressed. And when the clips in the folders could no longer bear the burden of additional poems, the poet would withdraw some and have them sewn into booklets. He died at seventy without having published a collected edition of his work, presumably because he did not consider it ready yet for that kind of permanent definition. He is reported to have said during his last days that he still had at least twenty-five poems to write, and his archive held a number that he apparently considered still in draft form.

This mode of publication, if it can be called that, suggests not only an unusual aesthetic asceticism—no interest at all in commerce and a total commitment to the craft of poetry—but also what George Seferis saw to be Cavafy's perception of his oeuvre as a lifelong work in progress, still incomplete at his death. If we accept Seferis's term, the work in progress begins in the crucial year 1910, when Cavafy published two poems that seem to have emerged from his acceptance of Alexandria as his inevitable home. In "The City," a type of "didactic" monologue that the poet adopted briefly, the poet's persona tells the poem's "you" that he should not look for things elsewhere because the city will always pursue him until he grows old in the same streets and same neighborhoods that have been his fate all these years (wasted years, in this case). And in "The Satrapy" the persona spells out what the poem's self-exiled "you" has come to know all too well: that his heart really longs for the Crowns of Laurel, the priceless acclaim, of his home city which he has too readily exchanged for "satrapies and things like that" in another country.

Two poems that Cavafy published the following year dramatize themes and attitudes that would become central to his work henceforth. In one of his finest poems, "The God Abandons Antony" (written in 1910), the persona's advice to Mark Antony in his last hours gives him occasion first of all for deifying Alexandria: Cavafy alters his source in Plutarch and Shakespeare by substituting his home city for the gods Dionysus and Hercules. We see that Cleopatra's Alexandria has become the god that Roman Antony finally chose to worship and that abandons him in his defeat. But as a city given him for pleasures which he proved worthy of accepting, he must now honor that gift by facing its going away without illusions and "full of courage." What has been called Cavafy's hedonistic bias becomes apparent in his choosing the "final delectation" of exquisite music as a sign of all the other delectations that the noble Roman came to know in the city he is now losing.

In the poem "Ithaka," another of Cavafy's finest that he gave a final draft in 1910, the poet again transforms his source, in this case Homer's account of Odysseus's return to his home island from the Trojan War. Cavafy's transforming is a variation on Dante's and Tennyson's handling of the same theme. Both these poets offered an Odysseus who arrived home after a long absence only to find Ithaka less than fully satisfying and who soon made plans to travel forth a second time. Cavafy answers his predecessors by having his persona tell the Odysseus figure that arriving in Ithaka is what he is destined for, and he must keep that always in mind: one's destiny, the inevitable end of the journey, is a thing to be faced for what it is, without illusions, as we saw in "The God Abandons Antony":

And if you find her poor, Ithaka won't have fooled you.
Wise as you will have become, so full of experience,
you will have understood by then what these Ithakas mean.

What Cavafy's Odysseus will have understood, in contrast
to Homer's nostalgic hero and even those dissatisfied and still-
hungry heroes of Cavafy's predecessors, is that the meaning of
Ithaka is in the voyage home that it inspired. It is not reaching
home or again escaping its limitations once there that should oc-
cupy Odysseus's spirit and his body so much as those elevated
thoughts and rare excitement that are a product of the voyage
back. This new perspective is what will free the voyager's soul of
the monsters and obstacles and even Homer's angry god
Poseidon, so that when the voyager reaches his Ithaka he will be
rich not with what Ithaka has to offer him on his return, but with
all that he has gained along the way, including his coming to
know that this Cavafian perspective on things, this unhurried devotion to pleasure and knowledge, is Ithaka's ultimate value.

The adventures and discoveries that are to keep Cavafy's
Odysseus entertained until old age take him to the heart of the
Alexandrian's only partially Hellenized world, not mainland
Greece and its neighboring islands, but new country for Homer's
hero, where he will take pleasure in the sensual properties of
Phoenician trading stations and learn from the scholars of Egyptian cities. What has been called Cavafy's hedonistic bias is again
clearly evident here, but equally important is what we might call
his diaspora bias. As the diaspora philosopher in "Going Back
Home from Greece" puts it, those Greeks who come from the
waters of Cyprus, Syria, and Egypt carry Asiatic affections and
feelings that are sometimes alien to Hellenism and that in any
case are not something to be ashamed of or covered up but hon-
ored as cause for pride.

In Cavafy's mythical world, racial purity is not only boring—as E. M. Forster once pointed out—but limiting, confining, especially among those for whom affections are crucial. Knowing oneself and admitting the truth of what one knows are also crucial, while affectation is ludicrous. And puritanism is equally ludicrous, whether the source be pagan or Christian—even if Cavafy chose to be particularly satirical of Julian the Apostate for attempting to introduce his excessively puritanical paganism into the diaspora regions where Christians had become well-established hedonists, with an abiding love for art, theater, language, and the pleasures of the flesh.

Cavafy's Alexandrian myth, created in the year "Ithaka" took its final form, was expanded during the years following to cover a broad world of Hellenism that included regions to the east and a stretch of time from Alexander's days to the fall of the Byzantine Empire. From the myth we learn that challenging one's destiny may give the gods an excuse to do one in before the journey's end, but so will a soul closed to those things that satisfy the spirit and the body. The myth teaches us what those things are: beautiful lovers given to sensual pleasure, imaginative creation of various kinds, mixed cultures—especially those mixed cultures dominated by the Greek language—remembered sensations from early love affairs, the value of both art and artifice, of spectacle, of politic theater. When, in the 1912 poem "Alexandrian Kings," Antony and Cleopatra make an attempt to impress Rome by taking their children out to the Alexandrian gymnasium to crown them with meaningless titles referring to regions they did not command—Armenia, Media, Parthia, Cilicia, Syria, Phoenicia—the politically shrewd Alexandrians "knew of course / that this was all mere words, all theater," but

> . . . the day was warm and poetic,
> the sky a pale blue,
> the Alexandrian Gymnasium
> a complete artistic triumph,
> the courtiers wonderfully sumptuous, . . .
> and the Alexandrians thronged to the festival
> full of enthusiasm, and shouted acclamations
> in Greek, and Egyptian, and some in Hebrew,
> charmed by the lovely spectacle—
> though they knew of course what all this was worth,
> what empty words they really were, these kingships.

Along with political shrewdness, Cavafy's myth celebrates
the virtues of historical perspicacity, of seeing things not only for
what they are but what they are likely to become, including the
inevitable reversals in history that finally teach one not so much
the moral as the tragic sense of life. And the myth teaches the virtues of irony. What becomes a major object of the poet's irony
throughout his mature work is the kind of excess that leads to
hubris, whether represented by the actions of pagans or Christians. We see this at the beginning of his work in progress in the
lyrical 1911 dramatic monologue, "Ionic," where a fourth-
century Christian speaker reveals that for all the violent effort on
the part of his fellow Christians to destroy the remnant paganism
of those days, the ancient gods do not die so easily and occasion-
ally reappear in the landscape they still love to show that it is potent with their life:

> That we've broken their statues,
> that we've driven them out of their temples,
> doesn't mean at all that the gods are dead.
> O land of Ionia, they're still in love with you,

their souls still keep your memory.
When an August dawn wakes over you,
your atmosphere is potent with their life,
And sometimes a young ethereal figure,
indistinct, in rapid flight,
wings across your hills.

Another example of Cavafy's balanced perspective is the poem that completed his work during his lifetime, "On the Outskirts of Antioch," written in 1932–33. Here we again find a fourth-century Christian speaker, resident of Syrian Antioch, who portrays Julian the Apostate as an excessively intolerant defender of the ancient gods—which he no doubt was—having a temper tantrum at the expense of the local Christians and their holy martyr Vavylas, buried in the precinct of the temple of Apollo at Daphni. Julian is depicted as shouting ". . . take him away immediately, this Vavylas. / You there, do you hear? He gets on Apollo's nerves. / Grab him, raise him at once, / dig him out, take him away, throw him out, / take him wherever you want. This isn't a joke." Vavylas is removed. And the Christian speaker offers this bit of sarcasm to conclude the poem:

And hasn't the temple done brilliantly since!
In no time at all a colossal fire
broke out, a terrible fire,
and both the temple and Apollo burned to nothing.

Ashes the idol: dirt to be swept away.

Julian exploded, and he spread it around—
What else could he do?—that we, the Christians,
had set the fire. Let him say so.

It hasn't been proved. Let him say so.
The essential thing is: he exploded.

The essential thing is that the Christian speaker has cast out Julian's pagan god—in spirit if not in fact—as mercilessly and fanatically as he depicts Julian's treatment of the martyr Vavylas. An eye for an eye; no charity here. And Cavafy's quiet irony satirizes both. Joseph Brodsky tells us in an illuminating review-essay on Cavafy that the poet "did not choose between paganism and Christianity but was swinging between them like a pendulum." I would modify the metaphor by suggesting that it is the speaking voice—in this case, voices—that does the swinging; Cavafy's perspective is what holds the pendulum in place, aloof from the action, not taking sides except when arrogance, fanaticism, intolerance, hubris, or other excess earns his irony.

One way that Cavafy chose to keep a certain distance from his speakers and establish a point of view that transcended the biased depiction of any given moment in history, especially in his later work, was by way of dramatic irony in the traditional sense. For this he had to count on the reader's familiarity with a specific historical context—not always easy in view of his predilection for the byways of history. The best of his dramatic monologues play subtly with this mode, which, there is good reason to believe, was influenced by his reading Robert Browning. The late poem "In the Year 200 B.C." is perhaps the most satisfying example. Here the speaker's attitude in narrating history that began 130 years before his day reflects the particular historical situation established by the title. He begins his monologue with some irony about the Spartans (Lacedaimonians) of 330 B.C. who refused to join Macedonian Alexander's great pan-Hellenic expedition because, according to the speaker, they weren't about to be led and ordered around in an expedition that didn't have a

Spartan king in command. As a result, they not only denied themselves the glory of taking part in Alexander's magnificent victories but had no claim to the great diaspora world that emerged from his conquests, here eulogized by the proud speaker:

> And from this marvelous pan-Hellenic expedition
> triumphant, brilliant in every way,
> celebrated on all sides, glorified
> as no other has ever been glorified,
> incomparable, we emerged:
> the great new Hellenic world.
>
> We the Alexandrians, the Antiochians,
> the Selefkians, and the countless
> other Greeks of Egypt and Syria,
> and those in Media, and Persia, and all the rest:
> with our far-flung supremacy,
> our flexible policy of judicious integration,
> and our Common Greek Language
> which we carried as far as Bactria, as far as the Indians.
>
> Talk about Lacedaimonians after that.

The dramatic irony here is that the speaker's celebration of Alexander's diaspora world—which Cavafy himself celebrated in earlier poems—comes just three years before the last of the Macedonian Philips was routed by the Romans at Cynoscephalae and just ten years before Antiochus III the Great was defeated at Magnesia, thus establishing Roman supremacy over the great new world that is eulogized so glowingly in "In the Year 200 B.C." Cavafy knows his history and counts on his reader to know more than the speaker can know, even if he speaks the truth as he sees it from his limited perspective: Alexander's victories did have the grand consequences he outlines. But only for a while, and that is the point. In the end one must in fact talk about the Spartans after all that, because their haughty view of themselves in 330 B.C. was followed by a decline that anticipates what will follow our speaker's rather haughty view of his history before its inevitable reversals under conquering Rome. This is the poet's unspoken perspective above the speaker's particular bias: the perspective of a poet-historian who sees a broader and necessarily more tragic pattern behind even those periods of historical greatness that best manifest the cultural values he believes in, here represented by "our flexible policy of judicious integration" and "our Common Greek Language."

A fundamental aspect of Cavafy's unique perspective on the world, to adopt Auden's phrase, is his capacity to act as a mostly unspoken conscience that makes us recognize any individual success and any moment of historical ascendancy as subject to reversal by the gods. It is a perspective that, without making its case overtly, serves to warn us against those excesses that lead to fanaticism, intolerance, or self-satisfied complacency and that finds wisdom and courage to reside in a recognition of human limitations, above all the inevitable fate of all things mortal.

Cavafy's erotic poems, whether set in ancient or contemporary Alexandria, are colored by the same tragic sense that we find in what he himself designated as his historical or philosophical poems (categories, along with the erotic, that, he reminds his reader, often merge). The love affairs depicted are sometimes uninhibited and sometimes thoroughly satisfying, especially when imagination plays a more active role than reality (as in "Half an Hour"), but they are often clouded by the lover's feeling that the pleasure is "fatal" or "illicit" or "tainted," in any case "condemned" by society and doomed to be transient:

> It wouldn't have lasted long anyway—
> the experience of years makes that clear.
> Even so, Fate did put an end to it a bit abruptly.
> It was soon over, that wonderful life. . . .
> ("In the Evening")

Yet however fated, the erotic life in Cavafy has its redeeming qualities, first of all in the intensity of its pleasures, as we see in the same poem ("how strong the scents were, / what a magnificent bed we lay in, / what pleasure we gave our bodies"), then in the intoxication that comes with remembering the experience years later, and most of all, in the new life that the experience finds in poetry:

> . . . Delight of flesh between
> those half-opened clothes;
> quick baring of flesh—the vision of it
> that has crossed twenty-six years
> and comes to rest now in this poetry.
> ("Comes to Rest")

Even in those poems dominated by a sense of degradation or loss on the part of the lovers, the poet often discovers in those lovers a sensual purity and physical beauty that deserve to be celebrated, especially in recollection. Memory becomes the means for preserving what was ephemeral, the means for fixing beauty that time has altered and for rediscovering through fantasy a sensuality that was fleeting, however passionate. And it is only through memory that the poet can hope to recreate the original shape of his eroticism and give it new life in his art. By the time the poet neared the end of his "work in progress," memory was shown to be the single avenue to some degree of permanence for those committed to the "Alexandrian" way of life as Cavafy conceived it, with its devotion to exquisite if transient pleasures, its love of the Greek language, its worship of beauty whatever the devotee's particular religion or moment in history.

The subtlest evocation of this theme is in the late poem "Myris: Alexandria, A.D. 340," longest of those in the "canon," a dramatic monologue in which the erotic and the historical are brilliantly fused. The drama opens with a typical Cavafian representation of conflicting ideologies: an unnamed pagan speaker attending the funeral of his Christian lover, Myris, both initiates in the "Alexandrian" way of life, the Christian "more devoted to pleasure than all of us," beautiful, and "with a perfect feel for Greek rhythm." As preparations for the funeral go forward, the pagan speaker becomes increasingly uneasy among the "precious carpets, and vessels in silver and gold," hearing prayers to Jesus and Mary that are unfamiliar to him. He begins to remember several occasions when his lover, who never spoke about his religion, nevertheless drew himself back from the group of initiates as they made certain pagan gestures. The speaker finds doubt setting in, and the drama now becomes a struggle between the influence of Christian ritual as performed by priests "praying loudly / for the young man's soul" and the influence of the lost passionate life that the two lovers had known—a struggle, finally, between Christian mystery and worldly memory:

> I noticed with how much diligence,
> how much intense concern
> for the forms of their religion, they were preparing

everything for the Christian funeral.
And suddenly an odd sensation
took hold of me. Indefinably I felt
as if Myris were going from me;
I felt that he, a Christian, was united
with his own people and that I was becoming
a stranger, a total stranger. I even felt
a doubt come over me: that I'd also been deceived by my passion
and had always been a stranger to him.
I rushed out of their horrible house,
rushed away before my memory of Myris
could be captured, could be perverted by their Christianity.

Memory, the resource that preserves and finally recreates the transient life of the senses, becomes, in the concluding lines of this monologue, the one relic of the speaker's passion, the one access to some life after death, that can challenge the Christian influence directed at capturing dead Myris's soul. The preservation through remembrance of the lost passionate life in its purity, untouched by doubt or alien intrusion, appears to be the ultimate act of faith for an Alexandrian hedonist of the Cavafian persuasion, here demonstrated by the speaker's rushing out of the Christian's house. That his act of faith and what it represents are finally as doomed as the speaker's own life, in contrast to the Christian expectation, does not diminish its poignancy—even when we remember that Cavafy himself, on his deathbed, was visited in the hospital by the patriarch of Alexandria, and though the poet refused to see him at first because the visit had been arranged without his knowledge, in the end consented and received the last sacraments.

Cavafy's mythical world presents us with an image of the good life—the life of exquisite sensuality, refined tastes, and mixed faiths—that more often than not carries within it the ripening prospect of its own death, yet in his work there appears to be no other life more worthy of celebration. And if there is a degree of ambivalence in his stance, this is consistent with his generally balanced, detached perspective. But it is not a cold detachment. The poet's sympathies, rarely expressed overtly, can usually be understood to go out to those who are the trapped victims of the ironies he perceives and dramatizes, especially to those fated souls with the courage to see themselves and their tragic circumstances for what they are. His mockery of self-delusion, in particular among the powerful, and his empathy with the outsider who faces his predicament without illusions are among the qualities that make him seem so contemporary. As ironist and realist, his vision is readily translatable into the language of contemporary experience; and the commitment to hedonism, to political skepticism, and to honest self-awareness that animate the special way of life at the heart of his myth anticipates the prevailing aura of our times.

Cavafy's perspective on the world was indeed unique in that it could be projected beyond the specific context of his individual creations, with judgment suspended and mercy granted, though not to the viciously power hungry, or puritanically arrogant, or the blindly self-deceived. And if translation into another language cannot completely capture all aspects of his unique tone of voice, particularly in those early poems that he rhymed strictly and in later poems where his sometimes quaint mixture of purist and demotic Greek was used to dramatic effect, my hope—in keeping with Auden's conviction—is that what comes through in English is more than enough to show why his deserves to be regarded as a major voice in the twentieth century.

EDMUND KEELEY

Poems

❖❖

The Horses of Achilles

When they saw Patroklos dead
—so brave and strong, so young—
the horses of Achilles began to weep;
their immortal nature was upset deeply
by this work of death they had to look at.
They reared their heads, tossed their long manes,
beat the ground with their hooves, and mourned
Patroklos, seeing him lifeless, destroyed,
now mere flesh only, his spirit gone,
defenseless, without breath,
turned back from life to the great Nothingness.

Zeus saw the tears of those immortal horses and felt sorry.
"At the wedding of Peleus," he said,
"I should not have acted so thoughtlessly.
Better if we hadn't given you as a gift,
my unhappy horses. What business did you have down there,
among pathetic human beings, the toys of fate.
You are free of death, you will not get old,
yet ephemeral disasters torment you.
Men have caught you up in their misery."
But it was for the eternal disaster of death
that those two gallant horses shed their tears.

Waiting for the Barbarians

What are we waiting for, assembled in the forum?

   The barbarians are due here today.

Why isn't anything happening in the senate?
Why do the senators sit there without legislating?

   Because the barbarians are coming today.
   What laws can the senators make now?
   Once the barbarians are here, they'll do the legislating.

Why did our emperor get up so early,
and why is he sitting at the city's main gate
on his throne, in state, wearing the crown?

   Because the barbarians are coming today
   and the emperor is waiting to receive their leader.
   He has even prepared a scroll to give him,
   replete with titles, with imposing names.

Why have our two consuls and praetors come out today
wearing their embroidered, their scarlet togas?
Why have they put on bracelets with so many amethysts,
and rings sparkling with magnificent emeralds?
Why are they carrying elegant canes
beautifully worked in silver and gold?

   Because the barbarians are coming today
   and things like that dazzle the barbarians.

Why don't our distinguished orators come forward as usual
to make their speeches, say what they have to say?

    Because the barbarians are coming today
    and they're bored by rhetoric and public speaking.

Why this sudden restlessness, this confusion?
(How serious people's faces have become.)
Why are the streets and squares emptying so rapidly,
everyone going home so lost in thought?

    Because night has fallen and the barbarians have not come.
    And some who have just returned from the border say
    there are no barbarians any longer.

And now, what's going to happen to us without barbarians?
They were, those people, a kind of solution.

Trojans

Our efforts are those of men prone to disaster;
our efforts are like those of the Trojans.
We just begin to get somewhere,
gain a little confidence,
grow almost bold and hopeful,

when something always comes up to stop us:
Achilles leaps out of the trench in front of us
and terrifies us with his violent shouting.

Our efforts are like those of the Trojans.
We think we'll change our luck
by being resolute and daring,
so we move outside ready to fight.

But when the great crisis comes,
our boldness and resolution vanish;
our spirit falters, paralyzed,
and we scurry around the walls
trying to save ourselves by running away.

Yet we're sure to fail. Up there,
high on the walls, the dirge has already begun.
They're mourning the memory, the aura of our days.
Priam and Hecuba mourn for us bitterly.

The City

You said: "I'll go to another country, go to another shore,
find another city better than this one.
Whatever I try to do is fated to turn out wrong
and my heart lies buried as though it were something dead.
How long can I let my mind moulder in this place?
Wherever I turn, wherever I happen to look,
I see the black ruins of my life, here,
where I've spent so many years, wasted them, destroyed them
     totally."

You won't find a new country, won't find another shore.
This city will always pursue you. You will walk
the same streets, grow old in the same neighborhoods,

will turn gray in these same houses.
You will always end up in this city. Don't hope for things
    elsewhere:
there is no ship for you, there is no road.
As you've wasted your life here, in this small corner,
you've destroyed it everywhere else in the world.

The Satrapy

Too bad that, cut out as you are
for grand and noble acts,
this unfair fate of yours
never offers encouragement, always denies you success;
that cheap habits get in your way,
pettiness, or indifference.
And how terrible the day you give in
(the day you let go and give in)
and take the road for Susa
and go to King Artaxerxes,
who, well-disposed, gives you a place at his court
and offers you satrapies and things like that—
things you don't want at all,
though, in despair, you accept them just the same.
You long for something else, ache for other things:
praise from the Demos and the Sophists,
that hard-won, that priceless acclaim—
the Agora, the Theatre, the Crowns of Laurel.
You can't get any of these from Artaxerxes,
you'll never find any of these in the satrapy,
and without them, what kind of life will you live?

The God Abandons Antony

When suddenly, at midnight, you hear
an invisible procession going by
with exquisite music, voices,
don't mourn your luck that's failing now,
work gone wrong, your plans
all proving deceptive—don't mourn them uselessly.
As one long prepared, and graced with courage,
say goodbye to her, the Alexandria that is leaving.
Above all, don't fool yourself, don't say
it was a dream, your ears deceived you:
don't degrade yourself with empty hopes like these.
As one long prepared, and graced with courage,
as is right for you who were given this kind of city,
go firmly to the window
and listen with deep emotion, but not
with the whining, the pleas of a coward;
listen—your final delectation—to the voices,
to the exquisite music of that strange procession,
and say goodbye to her, to the Alexandria you are losing.

Ionic

That we've broken their statues,
that we've driven them out of their temples,
doesn't mean at all that the gods are dead.
O land of Ionia, they're still in love with you,
their souls still keep your memory.
When an August dawn wakes over you,
your atmosphere is potent with their life,

and sometimes a young ethereal figure,
indistinct, in rapid flight,
wings across your hills.

Ithaka

As you set out for Ithaka
hope the voyage is a long one,
full of adventure, full of discovery.
Laistrygonians and Cyclops,
angry Poseidon—don't be afraid of them:
you'll never find things like that on your way
as long as you keep your thoughts raised high,
as long as a rare excitement
stirs your spirit and your body.
Laistrygonians and Cyclops,
wild Poseidon—you won't encounter them
unless you bring them along inside your soul,
unless your soul sets them up in front of you.

Hope the voyage is a long one.
May there be many a summer morning when,
with what pleasure, what joy,
you come into harbors seen for the first time;
may you stop at Phoenician trading stations
to buy fine things,
mother of pearl and coral, amber and ebony,
sensual perfume of every kind—
as many sensual perfumes as you can;
and may you visit many Egyptian cities
to gather stores of knowledge from their scholars.

Keep Ithaka always in your mind.
Arriving there is what you are destined for.
But do not hurry the journey at all.
Better if it lasts for years,
so you are old by the time you reach the island,
wealthy with all you have gained on the way,
not expecting Ithaka to make you rich.

Ithaka gave you the marvelous journey.
Without her you would not have set out.
She has nothing left to give you now.

And if you find her poor, Ithaka won't have fooled you.
Wise as you will have become, so full of experience,
you will have understood by then what these Ithakas mean.

Philhellene

Make sure the engraving is done skillfully.
The expression serious, majestic.
The diadem preferably somewhat narrow:
I don't like that broad kind the Parthians wear.
The inscription, as usual, in Greek:
nothing excessive, nothing pompous—
we don't want the proconsul to take it the wrong way:
he's always nosing things out and reporting back to Rome—
but of course giving me due honor.
Something very special on the other side:
some discus-thrower, young, good-looking.
Above all I urge you to see to it
(Sithaspis, for God's sake don't let them forget)

that after "King" and "Savior,"
they engrave "Philhellene" in elegant characters.
Now don't try to be clever
with your "where are the Greeks?" and "what things Greek
here behind Zagros, out beyond Phraata?"
Since so many others more barbarian than ourselves
choose to inscribe it, we will inscribe it too.
And besides, don't forget that sometimes
sophists do come to us from Syria,
and versifiers, and other triflers of that kind.
So we are not, I think, un-Greek.

Alexandrian Kings

The Alexandrians turned out in force
to see Cleopatra's children,
Kaisarion and his little brothers,
Alexander and Ptolemy, who for the first time
had been taken out to the Gymnasium,
to be proclaimed kings there
before a brilliant array of soldiers.

Alexander: they declared him
king of Armenia, Media, and the Parthians.
Ptolemy: they declared him
king of Cilicia, Syria, and Phoenicia.
Kaisarion was standing in front of the others,
dressed in pink silk,
on his chest a bunch of hyacinths,
his belt a double row of amethysts and sapphires,
his shoes tied with white ribbons

prinked with rose-colored pearls.
They declared him greater than his little brothers,
they declared him King of Kings.

The Alexandrians knew of course
that this was all mere words, all theater.

But the day was warm and poetic,
the sky a pale blue,
the Alexandrian Gymnasium
a complete artistic triumph,
the courtiers wonderfully sumptuous,
Kaisarion all grace and beauty
(Cleopatra's son, blood of the Lagids);
and the Alexandrians thronged to the festival
full of enthusiasm, and shouted acclamations
in Greek, and Egyptian, and some in Hebrew,
charmed by the lovely spectacle—
though they knew of course what all this was worth,
what empty words they really were, these kingships.

He Swears

He swears every now and then to begin a better life.
But when night comes with its own counsel,
its own compromises and prospects—
when night comes with its own power
of a body that needs and demands,
he goes back, lost, to the same fatal pleasure.

For Ammonis, Who Died at 29, in 610

Raphael, they're asking you to write a few lines
as an epitaph for the poet Ammonis:
something very tasteful and polished. You can do it,
you're the one to write something suitable
for the poet Ammonis, our Ammonis.

Of course you'll speak about his poems—
but say something too about his beauty,
about his subtle beauty that we loved.

Your Greek is always elegant and musical.
But we want all your craftsmanship now.
Our sorrow and our love move into a foreign language.
Pour your Egyptian feeling into the Greek you use.

Raphael, your verses, you know, should be written
so they contain something of our life within them,
so the rhythm, so every phrase clearly shows
that an Alexandrian is writing about an Alexandrian.

One of Their Gods

When one of them moved through the marketplace of Selefkia
just as it was getting dark—
moved like a young man, tall, extremely handsome,
with the joy of being immortal in his eyes,
with his black and perfumed hair—
the people going by would gaze at him,
and one would ask the other if he knew him,

if he was a Greek from Syria, or a stranger.
But some who looked more carefully
would understand and step aside;
and as he disappeared under the arcades,
among the shadows and the evening lights,
going toward the quarter that lives
only at night, with orgies and debauchery,
with every kind of intoxication and desire,
they would wonder which of Them it could be,
and for what suspicious pleasure
he had come down into the streets of Selefkia
from the August Celestial Mansions.

In the Evening

It wouldn't have lasted long anyway—
the experience of years makes that clear.
Even so, Fate did put an end to it a bit abruptly.
It was soon over, that wonderful life.
Yet how strong the scents were,
what a magnificent bed we lay in,
what pleasure we gave our bodies.

An echo from my days given to sensuality,
an echo from those days came back to me,
something of the fire of the young life we shared:
I picked up a letter again,
and I read it over and over till the light faded away.

Then, sad, I went out on to the balcony,
went out to change my thoughts at least by seeing

something of this city I love,
a little movement in the street and the shops.

Kaisarion

Partly to throw light on a certain period,
partly to kill an hour or two,
last night I picked up and read
a volume of inscriptions about the Ptolemies.
The lavish praise and flattery are much the same
for each of them. All are brilliant,
glorious, mighty, benevolent;
everything they undertake is full of wisdom.
As for the women of their line, the Berenices and Cleopatras,
they too, all of them, are marvelous.

When I'd verified the facts I wanted
I would have put the book away had not a brief
insignificant mention of King Kaisarion
suddenly caught my eye . . .

And there you were with your indefinable charm.
Because we know
so little about you from history,
I could fashion you more freely in my mind.
I made you good-looking and sensitive.
My art gives your face
a dreamy, an appealing beauty.
And so completely did I imagine you
that late last night,
as my lamp went out—I let it go out on purpose—

it seemed you came into my room,
it seemed you stood there in front of me, looking just as you
    would have
in conquered Alexandria,
pale and weary, ideal in your grief,
still hoping they might take pity on you,
those scum who whispered: "Too many Caesars."

Nero's Deadline

Nero wasn't worried at all when he heard
the utterance of the Delphic Oracle:
"Beware the age of seventy-three."
Plenty of time to enjoy himself still.
He's thirty. The deadline
the god has given him is quite enough
to cope with future dangers.

Now, a little tired, he'll return to Rome—
but wonderfully tired from that journey
devoted entirely to pleasure:
theaters, garden-parties, stadiums...
evenings in the cities of Achaia...
and, above all, the sensual delight of naked bodies...

So much for Nero. And in Spain Galba
secretly musters and drills his army—
Galba, the old man in his seventy-third year.

Since Nine O'Clock

Half past twelve. Time has gone by quickly
since nine o'clock when I lit the lamp
and sat down here. I've been sitting without reading,
without speaking. Completely alone in the house,
whom could I talk to?

Since nine o'clock when I lit the lamp
the shade of my young body
has come to haunt me, to remind me
of shut scented rooms,
of past sensual pleasure—what daring pleasure.
And it's also brought back to me
streets now unrecognizable,
bustling nightclubs now closed,
theaters and cafés no longer there.

The shade of my young body
also brought back the things that make us sad:
family grief, separations,
the feelings of my own people, feelings
of the dead so little acknowledged.

Half past twelve. How the time has gone by.
Half past twelve. How the years have gone by.

The Afternoon Sun

This room, how well I know it.
Now they're renting it, and the one next to it,

as offices. The whole house has become
an office building for agents, merchants, companies.

This room, how familiar it is.

Here, near the door, was the couch,
a Turkish carpet in front of it.
Close by, the shelf with two yellow vases.
On the right—no, opposite—a wardrobe with a mirror.
In the middle the table where he wrote,
and the three big wicker chairs.
Beside the window was the bed
where we made love so many times.

They must still be around somewhere, those old things.

Beside the window was the bed;
the afternoon sun fell across half of it.

. . . One afternoon at four o'clock we separated
for a week only . . . And then—
that week became forever.

Comes to Rest

It must have been one o'clock at night
or half past one.

A corner in the wine-shop
behind the wooden partition:
except for the two of us the place completely empty.

An oil lamp barely gave it light.
The waiter, on duty all day, was sleeping by the door.

No one could see us. But anyway,
we were already so aroused
we'd become incapable of caution.

Our clothes half opened—we weren't wearing much:
a divine July was ablaze.

Delight of flesh between
those half-opened clothes;
quick baring of flesh—the vision of it
that has crossed twenty-six years
and comes to rest now in this poetry.

Dareios

Phernazis the poet is at work
on the crucial part of his epic:
how Dareios, son of Hystaspis,
took over the Persian kingdom.
(It's from him, Dareios, that our glorious king,
Mithridatis, Dionysos and Evpator, descends.)
But this calls for serious thought; Phernazis has to analyze
the feelings Dareios must have had:
arrogance, maybe, and intoxication? No—more likely
a certain insight into the vanities of greatness.
The poet thinks deeply about the question.

But his servant, rushing in, cuts him short
to announce very serious news:
the war with the Romans has begun;
most of our army has crossed the borders.

The poet is dumbfounded. What a disaster!
How can our glorious king,
Mithridatis, Dionysos and Evpator,
bother about Greek poems now?
In the middle of a war—just think, Greek poems!

Phernazis gets all worked up. What bad luck!
Just when he was sure to distinguish himself
with his *Dareios,* sure to silence
his envious critics once and for all.
What a setback, terrible setback to his plans.

And if it's only a setback, that wouldn't be too bad.
But can we really consider ourselves safe in Amisos?
The town isn't very well fortified,
and the Romans are the most awful enemies.
Are we, Cappadocians, really a match for them?
Is it conceivable?
Are we now to pit ourselves against the legions?
Great gods, protectors of Asia, help us.

But through all his distress, all the turmoil,
the poetic idea comes and goes insistently:
arrogance and intoxication—that's the most likely, of course:
arrogance and intoxication are what Dareios must have felt.

A Byzantine Nobleman in Exile Composing Verses

The frivolous can call me frivolous.
I've always been most punctilious about
important things. And I insist
that no one knows better than I do
the Holy Fathers, or the Scriptures, or the Canons of the
    Councils.
Whenever he was in doubt,
whenever he had any ecclesiastical problem,
Botaniatis consulted me, me first of all.
But exiled here (may she be cursed, that viper
Irini Doukaina), and incredibly bored,
it is not altogether unfitting to amuse myself
writing six- and eight-line verses,
to amuse myself poeticizing myths
of Hermes and Apollo and Dionysos,
or the heroes of Thessaly and the Peloponnese;
and to compose the most strict iambics,
such as—if you'll allow me to say so—
the intellectuals of Constantinople don't know how to
    compose.
It may be just this strictness that provokes their disapproval.

From the School of the Renowned Philosopher

For two years he studied with Ammonios Sakkas,
but he was bored by both philosophy and Sakkas.

Then he went into politics.
But he gave that up. That Prefect was an idiot,

and those around him, somber-faced officious nitwits:
their Greek—poor fools—absolutely barbaric.

After that he became
vaguely curious about the Church: to be baptized
and pass as a Christian. But he soon
changed his mind: it would certainly have caused a row
with his parents, ostentatious pagans,
and—horrible thought—
they would have cut off at once
their extremely generous allowance.

But he had to do something. He began to haunt
the corrupt houses of Alexandria,
every secret den of debauchery.

In this fortune favored him:
he'd been given an extremely handsome figure.
And he enjoyed the divine gift.

His looks would last
at least another ten years. And after that?
Maybe he'll go back to Sakkas.
Or if the old man has died meanwhile,
he'll go to another philosopher or sophist:
there's always someone suitable around.

Or in the end he might possibly return
even to politics—commendably remembering
the traditions of his family,
duty toward the country,
and other resonant banalities of that kind.

In Despair

He lost him completely. And he now tries to find
his lips in the lips of each new lover,
he tries in the union with each new lover
to convince himself that it's the same young man,
that it's to him he gives himself.

He lost him completely, as though he never existed.
He wanted, his lover said, to save himself
from the tainted, unhealthy form of sexual pleasure,
the tainted, shameful form of sexual pleasure.
There was still time, he said, to save himself.

He lost him completely, as though he never existed.
Through fantasy, through hallucination,
he tries to find his lips in the lips of other young men,
he longs to feel his kind of love once more.

John Kantakuzinos Triumphs

He sees the fields that still belong to him:
the wheat, the animals, the trees laden with fruit;
and beyond them his ancestral home
full of clothes, costly furniture, silverware.

They'll take it all away from him—O God—they'll take it all
    away from him now.

Would Kantakuzinos show pity for him
if he went and fell at his feet? They say he's merciful,

very merciful. But those around him? And the army?—
Or should he fall down and plead before Lady Irini?

Fool that he was to get mixed up in Anna's party!
If only Lord Andronikos had never married her!
Has she ever done anything good, shown any humanity?
Even the Franks don't respect her any longer.
Her plans were ridiculous, all her plotting farcical.
While they were threatening everyone from Constantinople,
Kantakuzinos demolished them, Lord John demolished them.

And to think he'd planned to join Lord John's party!
And he would have done it, and would have been happy now,
a great nobleman still, his position secure,
if the bishop hadn't dissuaded him at the last moment
with his imposing hieratic presence,
his information bogus from beginning to end,
his promises, and all his drivel.

In a Township of Asia Minor

The news about the outcome of the sea-battle at Actium
was of course unexpected.
But there's no need for us to draft a new proclamation.
The name's the only thing that has to be changed.
There, in the concluding lines, instead of: "Having freed the
    Romans
from Octavius, that disaster,
that parody of a Caesar,"
we'll substitute: "Having freed the Romans
from Antony, that disaster, . . ."
The whole text fits very nicely.

"To the most glorious victor,
matchless in his military ventures,
prodigious in his political operations,
on whose behalf the township ardently wished
for Antony's triumph, . . . "
here, as we said, the substitution: "for Octavius Caesar's
      triumph,
regarding it as Zeus' finest gift—
to this mighty protector of the Greeks,
who graciously honors Greek customs,
who is beloved in every Greek domain,
who clearly deserves exalted praise,
and whose exploits should be recorded at length
in the Greek language, in both verse and prose,
in the *Greek language,* the vehicle of fame,"
et cetera, et cetera. It all fits brilliantly.

In the Tavernas

I wallow in the tavernas and brothels of Beirut.
I didn't want to stay
in Alexandria. Tamides left me;
he went off with the Prefect's son to earn himself
a villa on the Nile, a mansion in the city.
It wouldn't have been right for me to stay in Alexandria.
I wallow in the tavernas and brothels of Beirut.
I live a vile life, devoted to cheap debauchery.
The one thing that saves me,
like durable beauty, like perfume
that goes on clinging to my flesh, is this: Tamides,
most exquisite of young men, was mine for two years,
and mine not for a house or a villa on the Nile.

Days of 1896

He became completely degraded. His erotic tendency,
condemned and strictly forbidden
(but innate for all that), was the cause of it:
society was totally prudish.
He gradually lost what little money he had,
then his social standing, then his reputation.
Nearly thirty, he had never worked a full year—
at least not at a legitimate job.
Sometimes he earned enough to get by
acting the go-between in deals considered shameful.
He ended up the type likely to compromise you thoroughly
if you were seen around with him often.

But this isn't the whole story—that would not be fair.
The memory of his beauty deserves better.
There is another angle; seen from that
he appears attractive, appears
a simple, genuine child of love,
without hesitation putting,
above his honor and reputation,
the pure sensuality of his pure flesh.

Above his reputation? But society,
prudish and stupid, had it wrong.

In a Large Greek Colony, 200 B.C.

That things in the Colony are not what they should be
no one can doubt any longer,

and though in spite of everything we do go forward,
maybe—as more than a few believe—the time has come
to bring in a Political Reformer.

But here's the problem, here's the hitch:
they make a tremendous fuss
about everything, these Reformers.
(What a relief it would be
if no one ever needed them.) They probe everywhere,
question the smallest detail,
and right away think up radical changes
that demand immediate execution.

Also, they have a liking for sacrifice:
Get rid of that property;
your owning it is risky:
properties like those are exactly what ruin colonies.
Get rid of that income,
and the other connected with it,
and this third, as a natural consequence:
they are substantial, but what can one do?
the responsibility they create for you is damaging.

And as they proceed with their investigation,
they find an endless number of useless things to eliminate—
things that are, however, difficult to get rid of.

And when, all being well, they finish the job,
every detail now diagnosed and sliced away,
and they retire, also taking the wages due to them—
it will be a miracle if anything's left at all
after such surgical efficiency.

Maybe the moment has not yet arrived.
Let's not be too hasty: haste is a dangerous thing.
Untimely measures bring repentance.
Certainly, and unhappily, many things in the Colony are
    absurd.
But is there anything human without some fault?
And after all, you see, we do go forward.

A Prince from Western Libya

Aristomenis, son of Menelaos,
the Prince from Western Libya,
was generally liked in Alexandria
during the ten days he spent there.
As his name, his dress, modest, was also Greek.
He received honors gladly,
but he did not solicit them; he was unassuming.
He bought Greek books,
especially history and philosophy.
Above all he was a man of few words.
It got around that he must be a profound thinker,
and men like that naturally don't speak very much.

He was neither a profound thinker nor anything else—
just a piddling, laughable man.
He assumed a Greek name, dressed like the Greeks,
learned to behave more or less like a Greek;
and all the time he was terrified he would spoil
his reasonably good image
by coming out with barbaric howlers in Greek
and the Alexandrians, in their usual way,
would make fun of him, vile people that they are.

This was why he limited himself to a few words,
terribly careful of his syntax and pronunciation;
and he was driven almost out of his mind, having
so much talk bottled up inside him.

Myris: Alexandria, A.D. 340

When I heard the terrible news, that Myris was dead,
I went to his house, although I avoid
going to the houses of Christians,
especially during times of mourning or festivity.

I stood in the corridor. I didn't want
to go further inside because I noticed
that the relatives of the deceased looked at me
with obvious surprise and displeasure.

They had him in a large room,
and from the corner where I stood
I could catch a glimpse of it: all precious carpets,
and vessels in silver and gold.

I stood and wept in a corner of the corridor.
And I thought how our parties and excursions
would no longer be worthwhile without Myris;
and I thought how I'd no longer see him
at our wonderfully indecent night-long sessions
enjoying himself, laughing, and reciting verses
with his perfect feel for Greek rhythm;
and I thought how I'd lost forever
his beauty, lost forever
the young man I'd worshipped so passionately.

Some old women close to me were talking with lowered
    voices
about the last day he lived:
the name of Christ constantly on his lips,
his hand holding a cross.
Then four Christian priests
came into the room, and said prayers
fervently, and orisons to Jesus,
or to Mary (I'm not very familiar with their religion).

We'd known, of course, that Myris was a Christian,
known it from the very start,
when he first joined our group the year before last.
But he lived exactly as we did.
More devoted to pleasure than all of us,
he scattered his money lavishly on amusements.
Not caring what anyone thought of him,
he threw himself eagerly into night-time scuffles
when our group happened to clash
with some rival group in the street.
He never spoke about his religion.
And once we even told him
that we'd take him with us to the Serapeion.
But—I remember now—
he didn't seem to like this joke of ours.
And yes, now I recall two other incidents.
When we made libations to Poseidon,
he drew himself back from our circle and looked elsewhere.
And when one of us in his fervor said:
"May all of us be favored and protected
by the great, the sublime Apollo"—
Myris, unheard by the others, whispered: "not counting me."

The Christian priests were praying loudly
for the young man's soul.
I noticed with how much diligence,
how much intense concern
for the forms of their religion, they were preparing
everything for the Christian funeral.
And suddenly an odd sensation
took hold of me. Indefinably I felt
as if Myris were going from me;
I felt that he, a Christian, was united
with his own people and that I was becoming
a stranger, a total stranger. I even felt
a doubt come over me: that I'd also been deceived by my
    passion
and had always been a stranger to him.
I rushed out of their horrible house,
rushed away before my memory of Myris
could be captured, could be perverted by their Christianity.

To Have Taken the Trouble

I'm broke and practically homeless.
This fatal city, Antioch,
has devoured all my money:
this fatal city with its extravagant life.

But I'm young and in excellent health.
Prodigious master of things Greek,
I know Aristotle and Plato through and through,
poets, orators, or anyone else you could mention.
I have some idea about military matters

and friends among the senior mercenaries.
I also have a foot in the administrative world;
I spent six months in Alexandria last year:
I know (and this is useful) something about what goes on
        there—
the scheming of Kakergetis, his dirty deals, and the rest of it.

So I consider myself completely qualified
to serve this country,
my beloved fatherland, Syria.

Whatever job they give me,
I'll try to be useful to the country. That's my intention.
But if they frustrate me with their maneuvers—
we know them, those smart operators: no need to say more
        here—
if they frustrate me, it's not my fault.

I'll approach Zabinas first,
and if that idiot doesn't appreciate me,
I'll go to his rival, Grypos.
And if that imbecile doesn't take me on,
I'll go straight to Hyrkanos.

One of the three will want me anyway.

And my conscience is quiet
about my not caring which one I chose:
the three of them are equally bad for Syria.

But, a ruined man, it's not my fault.
I'm only trying, poor devil, to make ends meet.

The almighty gods ought to have taken the trouble
to create a fourth, an honest man.
I would gladly have gone along with him.

In the Year 200 B.C.

"Alexander, son of Philip, and the Greeks except the
    Lacedaimonians..."

We can very well imagine
how completely indifferent the Spartans would have been
to this inscription. "Except the Lacedaimonians"—
naturally. The Spartans
weren't to be led and ordered around
like precious servants. Besides,
a pan-Hellenic expedition without
a Spartan king in command
was not to be taken very seriously.
Of course, then, "except the Lacedaimonians."

That's certainly one point of view. Quite understandable.

So, "except the Lacedaimonians" at Granikos,
then at Issus, then in the decisive battle
where the terrible army
the Persians mustered at Arbela was wiped out:
it set out for victory from Arbela, and was wiped out.

And from this marvelous pan-Hellenic expedition,
triumphant, brilliant in every way,
celebrated on all sides, glorified

as no other has ever been glorified,
incomparable, we emerged:
the great new Hellenic world.

We the Alexandrians, the Antiochians,
the Selefkians, and the countless
other Greeks of Egypt and Syria,
and those in Media, and Persia, and all the rest:
with our far-flung supremacy,
our flexible policy of judicious integration,
and our Common Greek Language
which we carried as far as Bactria, as far as the Indians.

Talk about Lacedaimonians after that!

Days of 1908

He was out of work that year,
so he lived off card games,
backgammon, and borrowed money.

He was offered a job at three pounds a month
in a small stationery store,
but he turned it down without the slightest hesitation.
It wasn't suitable. It wasn't the right pay for him,
a reasonably educated young man, twenty-five years old.

He won two, maybe three dollars a day—sometimes.
How much could he expect to make out of cards and
    backgammon
in the cafés of his social level, working-class places,

however cleverly he played, however stupid the opponents he
   chose?
His borrowing—that was even worse.
He rarely picked up a dollar, usually no more than half that,
and sometimes he had to come down to even less.

For a week or so, sometimes longer,
when he managed to escape those horrible late nights,
he'd cool himself at the baths, and with a morning swim.

His clothes were a terrible mess.
He always wore the same suit,
a very faded cinnamon-brown suit.

O summer days of nineteen hundred and eight,
from your perspective
the cinnamon-brown suit was tastefully excluded.

Your perspective has preserved him
as he was when he took off, threw off,
those unworthy clothes, that mended underwear,
and stood stark naked, impeccably handsome, a miracle—
his hair uncombed, swept back,
his limbs a little tanned
from his morning nakedness at the baths and on the beach.

Growing in Spirit

He who hopes to grow in spirit
will have to transcend obedience and respect.
He will hold to some laws

but he will mostly violate
both law and custom, and go beyond
the established, inadequate norm.
Sensual pleasures will have much to teach him.
He will not be afraid of the destructive act:
half the house will have to come down.
This way he will grow virtuously into wisdom.

Going Back Home from Greece

Well, we're nearly there, Hermippos.
Day after tomorrow, it seems—that's what the captain said.
At least we're sailing our seas,
the waters of Cyprus, Syria, and Egypt,
the beloved waters of our home countries.
Why so silent? Ask your heart:
didn't you too feel happier
the farther we got from Greece?
What's the point of fooling ourselves?
That would hardly be properly Greek.

It's time we admitted the truth:
we are Greeks also—what else are we?—
but with Asiatic affections and feelings,
affections and feelings
sometimes alien to Hellenism.

It isn't right, Hermippos, for us philosophers
to be like some of our petty kings
(remember how we laughed at them
when they used to come to our lectures?)

who through their showy Hellenified exteriors,
Macedonian exteriors (naturally),
let a bit of Arabia peep out now and then,
a bit of Media they can't keep back.
And to what laughable lengths the fools went
trying to cover it up!

No, that's not at all right for us.
For Greeks like us that kind of pettiness won't do.
We must not be ashamed
of the Syrian and Egyptian blood in our veins;
we should really honor it, take pride in it.

Half an Hour

I never had you, nor I suppose
will I ever have you. A few words, an approach,
as in the bar the other day—nothing more.
It's sad, I admit. But we who serve Art,
sometimes with the mind's intensity,
can create—but of course only for a short time—
pleasure that seems almost physical.
That's how in the bar the other day—
mercifully helped by alcohol—
I had half an hour that was totally erotic.
And I think you understood this
and stayed slightly longer on purpose.
That was very necessary. Because
with all the imagination, with all the magic alcohol,
I needed to see your lips as well,
needed your body near me.

The Bandaged Shoulder

He said he'd hurt himself against a wall or had fallen down.
But there was probably some other reason
for the wounded, the bandaged shoulder.

Because of a rather abrupt gesture,
as he reached for a shelf to bring down
some photographs he wanted to look at,
the bandage came undone and a little blood ran.

I did it up again, taking my time
over the binding; he wasn't in pain
and I liked looking at the blood.
It was a thing of my love, that blood.

When he left, I found, in front of his chair,
a bloody rag, part of the dressing,
a rag to be thrown straight into the garbage;
and I put it to my lips
and kept it there a long while—
the blood of love against my lips.

On the Outskirts of Antioch

We in Antioch were astonished when we heard
what Julian was up to now.

Apollo had made things clear to him at Daphni:
he didn't want to give an oracle (as though we cared!),
he didn't intend to speak prophetically, unless

his temple at Daphni was purified first.
The nearby dead, he declared, got on his nerves.

There are many tombs at Daphni.
One of those buried there
was a triumphant and holy martyr Vavylas,
wonder and glory of our church.

It was him the false god hinted at, him he feared.
As long as he felt him near he didn't dare
pronounce his oracle: not a murmur.
(The false gods are terrified of our martyrs.)

Unholy Julian got worked up,
lost his temper and shouted: "Raise him, carry him out;
take him away immediately, this Vavylas.
You there, do you hear? He gets on Apollo's nerves.
Grab him, raise him at once,
dig him out, take him away, throw him out,
take him wherever you want. This isn't a joke.
Apollo said the temple has to be purified."

We took it, the holy relic, and carried it elsewhere.
We took it, we carried it away in love and in honor.

And hasn't the temple done brilliantly since!
In no time at all a colossal fire
broke out, a terrible fire,
and both the temple and Apollo burned to nothing.

Ashes the idol: dirt to be swept away.

Julian exploded, and he spread it around—
what else could he do?—that we, the Christians,
had set the fire. Let him say so.
It hasn't been proved. Let him say so.
The essential thing is—he exploded.

The Ships

From Imagination to the Blank Page. A difficult crossing, the
waters dangerous. At first sight the distance seems small, yet
what a long voyage it is, and how injurious sometimes for the
ships that undertake it.

The first injury derives from the highly fragile nature of the
merchandise that the ships transport. In the marketplaces of
Imagination most of the best things are made of fine glass and
diaphanous tiles, and despite all the care in the world, many
break on the way, and many break when unloaded on the shore.
Moreover, any such injury is irreversible, because it is out of the
question for the ship to turn back and take delivery of things
equal in quality. There is no chance of finding the same shop that
sold them. In the marketplaces of Imagination, the shops are
large and luxurious but not long-lasting. Their transactions are
short-lived, they dispose of their merchandise quickly and immediately liquidate. It is very rare for a returning ship to find the
same exporters with the same goods.

Another injury derives from the capacity of the ships. They
leave the harbors of the opulent continents fully loaded, and
then, when they reach the open sea, they are forced to throw out
a part of the load in order to save the whole. Thus, almost no
ship manages to carry intact as many treasures as it took on. The
discarded goods are of course those of the least value, but it hap-

pens sometimes that the sailors, in their great haste, make mistakes and throw precious things overboard.

And upon reaching the white paper port, additional sacrifices are necessary. The customs officials arrive and inspect a product and consider whether they should allow it to be unloaded; some other product is not permitted ashore; and some goods they admit only in small quantities. A country has its laws. Not all merchandise has free entry, and contraband is strictly forbidden. The importation of wine is restricted, because the continents from which the ships come produce wines and spirits from grapes that grow and mature in more generous temperatures. The customs officials do not want these alcoholic products in the least. They are highly intoxicating. They are not appropriate for all palates. Besides, there is a local company that has the monopoly in wine. It produces a beverage that has the color of wine and the taste of water, and this you can drink the day long without being affected at all. It is an old company. It is held in great esteem, and its stock is always overpriced.

Still, let us be pleased when the ships enter the harbor, even with all these sacrifices. Because, after all, with vigilance and great care, the number of broken or discarded goods can be reduced during the course of the voyage. Also, the laws of the country and the customs regulations, though oppressive in large measure, are not entirely prohibitive, and a good part of the cargo gets unloaded. Furthermore, the customs officials are not infallible: some of the merchandise gets through in mislabeled boxes that say one thing on the outside and contain something else; and, after all, some choice wines are imported for select symposia.

Something else is sad, very sad. That is when certain huge ships go by with coral decorations and ebony masts, with great white and red flags unfurled, full of treasures, ships that do not even approach the harbor either because all of their cargo is forbidden or because the harbor is not deep enough to receive them. So they continue on their way. A favorable wind fills their silk sails, the sun burnishes the glory of their golden prows, and they sail out of sight calmly, majestically, distancing themselves forever from us and our cramped harbor.

Fortunately, these ships are very scarce. During our lifetime we see two or three of them at most. And we forget them quickly. Equal to the radiance of the vision is the swiftness of its passing. And after a few years have gone by, if—as we sit passively gazing at the light or listening to the silence—if someday certain inspiring verses return by chance to our mind's hearing, we do not recognize them at first and we torment our memory trying to recollect where we heard them before. With great effort the old remembrance is awakened, and we recall that those verses are from the song chanted by the sailors, handsome as the heroes of the *Iliad,* when the great, the exquisite ships would go by on their way—who knows where.

(*Translated by Edmund Keeley and Dimitri Gondicas*)

Notes

❖❖

In the notes that follow, "written" designates the date of composition, when known. "Rewritten" indicates that the poem was actually recast by Cavafy in terms of both diction and sometimes meter, not merely corrected in places, as was often the case with poems even after publication of their "definitive" versions. The term "printed" is used instead of "published" whenever the poem was first privately printed by Cavafy, usually in broadsheets, and later published in a periodical or literary annual. For further comment on these notes, see the "Editor's Introduction to the Notes" in *C. P. Cavafy: Collected Poems,* revised edition, Princeton University Press, 1992.

The Horses of Achilles. Written 1896, published 1897. The poem is rhymed in the original. Patroklos was the close friend of Achilles, the son of Peleus and Thetis (for the poem's source, see Homer, *Iliad* 17.437ff.).

Waiting for the Barbarians. Written 1898, printed 1904. An imaginary scene in a conventional "decadent" Roman setting. According to Cavafy's comment on the poem, the barbarians here are a symbol; consequently, "the emperor, the senators and the orators are not necessarily Roman."

Trojans. Written 1900, published 1907. Priam and Hecuba were king and queen of Troy at the time of the Trojan War.

The City. Written 1894, published 1910. The poem is rhymed in the original, with mostly homophonous rhymes. According to Cavafy's thematic arrangement of his poems (see the appendix to the editor's introduction in *C. P. Cavafy: Collected Poems*), "The City" and "The Satrapy" are the twin portals to his mature poetry at least up to 1916.

The Satrapy. Perhaps first written 1903, written (or rewritten) 1905, published 1910. A satrapy was a Persian province governed by a satrap, under the ancient monarchy. In spite of the reference to King Artaxerxes (possibly the first of the three Persian monarchs of that name: 464–424 B.C.), Cavafy is reported to have said that the anonymous protagonist should not necessarily be identified with Themistokles or Dimaratos, who had both been honorably received by a Persian king as political refugees, or indeed any politician, but that he symbolizes, rather, an artist or possibly a scientist. Susa was the capital of Persia under the Achaemenid dynasty (c. 645–330 B.C.).

The God Abandons Antony. Written 1910, published 1911. The title is a quotation from Plutarch's *Life of Antony,* 75. Mark Antony believed himself to be under the special protection of the god Dionysus (see also Shakespeare, *Antony and Cleopatra* 4.3, where the god who abandons Antony is Hercules).

Ionic. Perhaps first written 1886, first version published 1896, rewritten 1905, final version published 1911.

Ithaka. A first, very different version written in 1894, final version written 1910, published 1911. The Laistrygonians and the Cyclops were cannibal giants encountered by Odysseus on his homeward journey to his native island of Ithaka.

Philhellene. Written 1906, published 1912. The scene and characters are imaginary. The speaker is some petty Eastern monarch who gives instructions to Sithaspis (probably a courtier) about a coin to be minted. Zagros was the name of a range of mountains dividing Media from Assyria and Susiana in Asia Minor. Phraata, a city of Media, was the winter residence of the Parthian kings.

Alexandrian Kings. Written and published in 1912. The regal debut of Cleopatra's children was stage-managed by Mark Antony in 34 B.C. Alexander and Ptolemaios Philadelphos were Antony's sons, whereas Kaisarion was the son of Julius Caesar. The youngest of these so-called kings was barely two years old and Kaisarion only fourteen. Four years later Antony and Cleopatra committed suicide, Kaisarion was executed, and the younger children were taken as hostages to Rome.

He Swears. Written 1905, printed 1915.

For Ammonis, Who Died at 29, in 610. Written 1915, printed 1917. The poem is loosely rhymed in the original. Ammonis, an Egyptian, and Raphael, a Copt, are both fictional characters. The date coincides with the beginning of Mohammed's career as a prophet.

One of Their Gods. Written 1899, printed 1917. The scene is set in one of several Hellenistic cities called Selefkia, of which the most splendid by far was Selefkia on Tigris, founded c. 312 B.C. by Selefkos I Nicator as the capital of his empire.

In the Evening. Written 1916, printed 1917. The poem is rhymed in the original and includes several homophonous rhymes.

Kaisarion. Written 1914, printed 1918. Kaisarion, i.e., "Little Caesar," or Ptolemy XVI, was the son of Julius Caesar and was Cleopatra's eldest child. In 34 B.C., Mark Antony conferred on him the title "King of Kings." After Antony's defeat, his victorious opponent, Gaius Julius Caesar Octavianus (i.e., the future emperor Augustus), who was Caesar's adopted son, ordered the execution of Kaisarion. This execution was the practical result of political advice paraphrasing an expression of the *Iliad* (2.204): "It is not a good thing to have many Caesars..."

Nero's Deadline. Written 1915, published 1918. In the spring of A.D. 68, Servius Sulpicius Galba (c. 3–69), then Roman governor of Eastern Spain, was invited by the army to replace the emperor Nero, who committed suicide shortly thereafter. Nero's visit to Achaia (i.e., Greece), during which he consulted the oracle, took place one year earlier.

Since Nine O'Clock. Written 1917, printed 1918. For the last twenty-five years of his life, Cavafy lived alone in Alexandria in the famous apartment on Rue Lepsius. His reference to "family grief" includes the deaths of his father (1870) and mother (1899), and of his brothers Peter (1891), George (1900), Aristeidis (1902), and Alexander (1905).

The Afternoon Sun. Written 1918, printed 1919. The poem is loosely rhymed in the original, and in the original, the sex of the former tenant of the room remains ambiguous.

Comes to Rest. Written 1918, printed 1919.

Dareios. Written 1917, printed 1920. The scene and the timorous poet Phernazis (a Persian name), both fictitious, are probably set in 74 B.C., in the strategically and commercially important city of Amisos, on the coast of Pontos (Black Sea), which fell to the Romans in 71 B.C. Dareios I (521–486 B.C.) was, after Cyrus the Great (559–529 B.C.), the greatest of the Achaemenid kings of Persia; in European history he is chiefly known for the defeat of his invading force at Marathon in 490 B.C. The actual circumstances of his rise to the throne of Persia are obscure and suspicious; therefore Phernazis, for their poetic treatment, faces a choice between historical truth, courtly caution, and psychological plausibility. Mithridatis VI Evpator ("The Good Father") was the semihellenized Persian king of Pontos (120–63 B.C.). Cicero designated him the greatest of all rulers after Alexander and the most formidable opponent of Rome in the East. He ascended to the throne in c. 115 B.C., jointly with his brother, whom he subsequently killed. In 74 B.C., he launched the Third Mithridatic War against the numerically inferior Romans in Bithynia. Defeated by Lucullus and Pompey in 66 B.C., he was overthrown by his own son, Pharnacis, who drove him to suicide.

A Byzantine Nobleman in Exile Composing Verses. Written 1921, printed 1921. The poem is sporadically rhymed in the original. The anonymous protagonist is a fictitious character, perhaps modeled on (but not identifiable with) the Byzantine emperor Michael VII, dethroned in 1081 by Alexios I Komninos, husband of Irini Doukaina (1066–1123).

From the School of the Renowned Philosopher. Written 1921, printed 1921. The anonymous protagonist is imaginary. The poem is set shortly before the death of Ammonios Sakkas (A.D. 243), the "Socrates of Neoplatonism," who taught in Alexandria and was said to have had Plotinus and the philosopher Origen among his disciples.

In Despair. Written 1923, printed 1923. The poem is loosely rhymed in the original.

John Kantakuzinos Triumphs. Printed 1924. The poem is rhymed in the original and set in the year 1347. The anonymous protagonist is fictional. When the Byzantine emperor Andronikos III Palaiologos died (1341), John Kantakuzinos, a wealthy favorite of his, was appointed regent. This led to an open clash between him and the widow of Andronikos, Anna of Savoy, mother of the eleven-year-old heir to the throne, John V. Although of French origin, Anna was supported by the patriarch of Constantinople. In 1347, Kantakuzinos, assisted by rich land-owners of Thrace and Thessaly, "triumphed" in his struggle. He was crowned joint emperor with his wife, Irini Assan, granddaughter of the tsar of Bulgaria, John III.

In a Township of Asia Minor. Printed 1926. The scene and the decree, both imaginary, are set in 31 B.C.

In the Tavernas. Printed 1926. The poem is sporadically rhymed in the original. The characters are imaginary.

Days of 1896. Written 1925, printed 1927. The poem is sporadically rhymed in the original.

In a Large Greek Colony, 200 B.C. Printed 1928. The poem is loosely rhymed in the original. The date in the title places this geographically undetermined Greek colony at the hinge of the Hellenistic period: three years before the battle of Cynoscephalae, where Philip V of Macedonia was crushingly defeated by the Romans, and ten years before the battle of Magnesia.

A Prince from Western Libya. Printed 1928. The protagonist and the situation are imaginary but by no means atypical. Libya was the Greek name for Africa in general.

Myris: Alexandria, A.D. 340. Printed 1929. The protagonist and scene are imaginary. The date places them in a time of great political and religious upheaval: civil strife between the sons of Constantine the Great, and religious clashes between the supporters of Arios and Athanasios in Alexandria, resulting in the latter's banishment to Rome. The Serapeion was the famous temple of Serapis (or Sarapis) in Alexandria, first built by Ptolemy Sotir c. 300 B.C., then splendidly rebuilt by Ptolemy III Evergetes (246–221 B.C.) and destroyed by the emperor Theodosius in A.D. 391. Serapis was not one of the ancient Egyptian gods but a syncretic combination of Osiris and Apis, with elements of Zeus, Dionysus, Pluto, and Asclepius. His official worship as patron of Alexandria was promoted by the Ptolemies, and his priests were mostly Greeks.

To Have Taken the Trouble. Printed 1930. The anonymous protagonist is a fictional character placed by Cavafy between 128 and 123 B.C. Kakergetis ("Malefactor") was the nickname of Ptolemy VIII Evergetis ("Benefactor"), also dubbed Physkon ("Bladder"), father of Ptolemy IX Sotir, commonly known as Lathyros ("Chickpea"). Zabinas ("Slave") was the nickname of Alexander II, the alleged son of the adventurer Alexander Valas, who usurped the throne of Syria (128–123 B.C.) with the help of Ptolemy VIII and was killed by Antiochos VIII Grypos ("Hooknose"). John Hyrkanos I, son of Simon Maccabaius, was king of Judaea from 134 to 104 B.C. and naturally profited from the feuds raging around the throne of Syria.

In the Year 200 B.C. Probably first written in 1916, printed in 1931. The title places the poem at the optimum moment of the decline of Hellenism: some 130 years after Alexander's victories, and three years before the battle of Cynoscephalae, where Philip V, the last of the Macedonian Philips, was crushingly defeated by the Romans. It is also ten years before the defeat of Antiochus III the Great at Magnesia, which marked the Roman conquest of "the great new Hellenic world" extolled in the poem. The opening line quotes from the dedicatory inscription which Alexander the Great ordered to be engraved on the three hundred Persian panoplies he sent to the Athenian Parthenon. Granikos, Issus, and Arbela were the three battles (334, 333, and 331 B.C.) that decided Alexander's Persian campaign. Concerning the stubborn refusal of the Lacedaimonians ("Spartans") to participate in that campaign, it is worth remembering that they had lost, since 371 B.C., their military supremacy to the Thebans, who were eventually crushed in 338 B.C. by the Macedonians. Indeed, by the third century B.C., the fighting power of the Lacedaimonians had dwindled to no more than seven hundred men, owing to the unwillingness of their kings to adapt their antiquated constitution to the new historical and social circumstances. The "Common Greek Language" (or *Koine*), based on the Attic dialect, became, for at least six hundred years, the international language of both the East and Christendom. Bactria was a satrapy between northern Afghanistan and southern Uzbekistan; it remained under Greek cultural influence until 140 B.C.

Days of 1908. Probably first written in 1921, printed 1932. The poem is loosely rhymed in the original.

Growing in Spirit. Probably written in 1903. This poem and the three that follow it in this selection were first published in the editor's collection of "unpublished poems," *Anekdota Poiemata,* Athens, 1968. The poem is rhymed in the original, and the Greek title literally means "Invigoration."

Going Back Home from Greece. Written 1914, published 1968. The scene and the anonymous speaker are fictitious. His interlocutor, Hermippos, could be either the third-century B.C. biographer or the grammarian of the time of Trajan and Hadrian (A.D. 98–138).

Half an Hour. Written 1917, published 1968.

The Bandaged Shoulder. Written 1919, published 1968.

On the Outskirts of Antioch. Almost certainly written between November 1932 and April 1933. Although prepared for the printer by Cavafy before his death, this poem appeared for the first time in the posthumous edition of 1935 and has been included ever since in the *corpus* of the published poems (sometimes called "the canon"). Vavylas—better known as St. Babylas—bishop of Antioch (c. 237–250) and martyr, had been reburied in the precinct of the temple and oracle of Apollo, in the grove of Daphni (a suburb of Antioch), at the initiative of Julian's half brother Gallus. The priests of Apollo abandoned the temple, which they considered to have been polluted by this burial, and the Christians built a church over Vavylas' tomb. When Julian arrived in Antioch (July 362), he gave orders for the church to be demolished, for Vavylas' bones to be carried back to their original grave, and for the ritual purification of the place. On October 22, 362, the roof of the temple and the internationally famous statue of Apollo were destroyed by a fire that was attributed to the vengeance of the Christians.

The Ships. This early prose poem, one of the very few that Cavafy wrote, was translated by Edmund Keeley and Dimitri Gondicas and published in English for the fist time in *Antaeus,* Fall, 1994. The translators' note indicates that it is among the unpublished works found in the Cavafy archive and was first published in Athens in 1986 by George Savidis, who estimates the date of composition to be between 1895 and 1896. Only a few poems in the so-called Cavafy canon have been assigned an earlier date of composition, though one of the most famous poems in the canon, "Waiting for the Barbarians," was written just two years later. The language of "The Ships" ("Ta Ploia") is fairly strict purist Greek, more formal and stilted than the mixed purist and demotic language of Cavafy's maturest work.

About the Editor

❖❖

Edmund Keeley was born in Damascus, Syria, of American parents and lived in Canada and Greece before his family settled in Washington, D.C. He studied at Princeton and Oxford, and taught Creative Writing and Hellenic Studies at Princeton until his retirement in 1994 as Straut Professor of English Emeritus. He is the author of fifteen volumes of poetry in translation, five volumes of non-fiction, and six novels, most recently *School for Pagan Lovers*. His fiction won the Rome Prize of the American Academy of Arts and Letters, a Guggenheim Fellowship, and selection by the PEN/NEA Fiction Syndicate. His translations received the Harold Morton Landon Award of the Academy of American Poets and the European Community's First European Prize for the Translation of Poetry. He has served as President of PEN American Center and twice as President of the Modern Greek Studies Association, of which he was a founding member. With his wife, Mary, he lives part of the year in Princeton and part in Athens, Greece.